Creative Mind

Tapping *the* Power Within

Creative Mind

Tapping *the* Power Within

Ernest S. Holmes

SQUAREONE
CLASSICS

Cover Design: Phaedra Mastrocola
Typesetting: Gary A. Rosenberg
Series Consultant: Skip Whitson
Printer: Paragon Press, Honesdale, PA

Square One Publishers
Garden City Park, NY 11040
(516) 535-2010
www.squareonepublishers.com

Library of Congress Cataloging-in-Publication Data

Holmes, Ernest, 1887–1960.
  Creative mind : tapping the power within / Ernest S. Holmes.
    p. cm. — (Square One classics)
Originally published: 3rd ed., rev. Los Angeles, Calif. : Science of
Mind Pub., 1998.
Includes index.
  ISBN 0-7570-0039-8 (pbk.)
  1. United Church of Religious Science—Doctrines. 2. New Thought.
I. Title. II. Series.
  BP605.U53 H634 2002
  299'.93—dc21
                                        2001008052

Contents

PART TWO ❧ PRACTICE

Introduction

THE HAND OF ETERNAL PROGRESS is brushing the cobwebs from the corridors of time and is again revealing to the human race the mysteries of being. As there is "nothing new under the sun," the searchlight of Truth is bringing to light only what has been known to the few in all generations. The time has now come when the few must become the many. The whole world, from the least to the greatest, must know the Truth, so that man may understand the great laws that govern his life. He must learn to control his own destiny, to heal his own body and bring happiness to his own soul. Ignorance must vanish and understanding must be ushered in. Man is no longer to be governed by anything outside himself. Creeds, doctrines, churches, institutions, organizations, governments are all being changed to give place to the realization of the individual. There is a power in and through all that is working this great transformation. All that will not measure up to the standard must fall by its own weight; all that is in line with the Truth must still prosper. The time is at hand; we are in the greatest age of all history; we are in the age of the unifying of all people and all things into the "Ever Present One." "The temple not made with hands" is now being silently built by the emancipated souls of this planet.

This little book is an attempt to explain what each soul must discover for himself, that he stands in the midst of an eternal creative power which presses itself around his own thought, and casts back to him glorified all that he thinks. If it awakens within the consciousness of one single individual the realization that the mind of the Universe (which is the only mind that there is) is his own mind; that the creative power of this mind is his also; that the manifestation of this mind is his own individuality; that the love and power and peace of this mind is within himself, it will not be written in vain. May it then do much in simplifying and bringing to light some of the deeper mysteries and meanings of life.

Part One

Principles

In the Beginning

"*I*N THE BEGINNING, GOD!*" Clear and expressive are these words. In the beginning, God only. No manifest universe! No system of planets! Nothing of form or life, of brute or man! God was the Spirit of All that was to be, but He had not yet moved upon the waters. Then this All-Being moved, or began to create. *Where* did Spirit move, upon *what* did It move to create; where did It get a pattern; what means or power did It employ; through what agencies did It work? In short, what is the world, ourselves included, made out of, and how did we and all else come into being? These questions correctly answered would solve the problem of being and set men free. Let us consider.

The Spirit was all; there was nothing else but Itself. All-Inclusive, Everywhere, Infinite. This All-Spirit could not have had the impulse to move unless It were self-conscious, therefore the Spirit is the Power that knows Itself; It is accordingly All-Knowing as well as All-Present. Being one, undivided, whatever It knows, It knows all over instantly. We find then that the Spirit operates through self knowing. It moves, and that inner movement must be one of Infinite Power, moving upon Itself—since It is all—and with a definite purpose. The Spirit, then, moves upon Itself, and makes out of Itself all that is made. In other words, what we see comes from what we do not see, through some inner intelligence at work, which knows there is no power but Itself. "The things that are seen are not made of the things that do appear." The only possible operation of intelligence is thought, or "The Word." So all things were made by the Word, and "Without the Word was not anything made that hath been made." How simple the process of creation when we understand it. The Spirit speaks—and since there is nothing but the Spirit and it is All-Power, it has only to speak and it is done; "The Word was with God and the Word was God."

From the Word, then, comes forth all that appears. Each life, human or divine, each manifestation is a different kind of word coming into expression. The great fact to dwell upon is that Spirit needs nothing to help It; It is self-conscious and has all power and all ability to do whatever It wishes to accomplish. It operates simply by speaking.

It is hard to get a clear concept of this great Ceaseless Cause, this something from which all things come; at times we get into a maze of confusion when we attempt to realize what the Spirit means. It is then that we should think of It as the great reason behind everything. Being

all-knowledge It must know Itself, and must know everything It creates; so It knows us and It knows everyone.
Since It is All-Presence we can contact anywhere and will
never have to go to some particular spot to find It. As It
is All-Knowing and operates through the power of the
Word, It knows everything we think. Just how It creates
we cannot know and need not attempt to understand, for
whatever this process of creation is, we find it is always an
inner thought process. We should keep this in mind—the
Spirit makes all things out of Itself. Everything comes
into being without effort, and when *we* exert ourselves
we are not in accord with the Creative Spirit in the way
in which It works. The impulse of the Spirit to move
must be caused by a desire to express what It feels Itself
to be—Beauty, Form, Color, Life, Love and Power. All
things else we find in the manifest universe are attributes
of the Spirit, and are caused to spring into being through
the Word, because the Spirit wants to enjoy Itself.

We find, then, that the Word, which is the inner activity of thought, comes first in the creative series, and all
else comes from the effect of the Word operating upon a
universal substance. If the Word precedes all else, then
the Word is what we are looking for, and when we get it
we shall have what the world has sought from time imme-
morial. We must, if we wish to prove the power of the
Spirit in our lives, look not to outside things or effects,
but to the Word alone. The human eye sees and the
human hand touches only that which is an effect. Un-

seen law controls everything; but this Law also is an effect; Law did not make itself; the Law is not intelligence or causation. Before there can be a Law there must be something that acts, and the Law is the way it acts; it is intelligence. "In the beginning was the Word." This Word or the activity of the Spirit, is the cause of the law, and the law in its place is the cause of the thing, and the thing is always an effect; that is, it did not make itself; it is a result. The Word always comes first in the creative series; "The Word was with God and the Word was God" and the Word *still is God.*

When we realize that man is like God (and he could not be otherwise, being made out of God), we will realize that his word also has power. If there is but One Mind then it follows that *our word, our thought* is the activity of that One Mind *in our consciousness;* the power that holds the planets in their place is the same power that flows through man. We must place the Word where it belongs, whether it is the word of God in the Universe or the word of man in the individual; it is always first, before all else, in the beginning. The real sequence is this: Cause, Spirit, Intelligence, God; the Word, the activity of Intelligence; the effect, or the visible thing, whether it is a planet or a peanut. All are made out of the same thing.

What we need to do is to learn how to use the word so that all will come to see that they are creative centers within themselves.

A Principle That
Can Be Proven

*K*NOWING THAT MIND IS, WE HAVE a principle that is absolute; it is exact; it is going to correspond to our thinking about it. The first great necessity is to believe this; without belief we can do nothing. This is the reason Jesus said, "It is done unto you even as you have believed." Always it is done unto people as they believe, and there is Something that does it which never fails.

We must believe that our word is formed upon and around by this creative Mind; for instance, we wish to create activity in our business; we believe that our word is law about that thing, and there is something that takes our thought and executes it for us. If we have accepted the fact that all is mind and that the thought is the thing, we shall see at once that our word is the power behind the thing, and that it depends upon the word or thought that we are sending out. (See *Creative Mind and Success* by the author.)

So plastic is mind, so receptive, that the slightest thought makes an impression upon it. People who think many kinds of thought must expect to receive a confused manifestation in their lives. If a gardener plants a thousand kinds of seeds, he will get a thousand kinds of plants; it is the same in mind.

The Word
Going Forth

*S*INCE THIS IS TRUE, EVERYTHING depends upon our mental concepts. "As a man thinketh in his heart, so is he"; the Bible reiterates this statement telling us many times of the creative power of thought; Jesus taught nothing else; He said, "The words which I speak unto you, they are Spirit and they are life."

The Centurion coming to Jesus recognized the power of the word spoken by the latter. He said, "I also am one in authority"; but his authority was on the physical plane, and he saw that Jesus had authority on a Spiritual plane, for he said, "Speak the word only."

The Bible also tells us that the word is not afar off but in our own mouth. It is neither here nor there; it is within every living soul. We must take the responsibility for our own lives. All must awake to the facts that they have absolute control over their lives, and that nothing can happen by chance. Then they will have a broader concept of God, a greater tolerance for their neighbor, and a greater realization of their own divine nature. What a relief from strenuous labor; no more struggle or strife.

"Be still and know that I am God, and beside me there is none other." The Spirit being all there is, we cannot conceive of anything that can hinder its working. When the Spirit has spoken, the Word becomes Law, for before the Law is the Word; It precedes all else. First is Absolute Intelligence, All-Power, All-Presence, All-Causation; then the movement upon itself through the power of the Word; then the Word becoming Law; the Law producing the thing and holding it in place.

So long as the Word exists the thing will exist, for since the Word is All-Power there is nothing beside It. "I Am that I Am, and beside me there is none other." This "I Am" is Spirit, God, All. There is no physical explanation for anything in the universe; all causation is Spirit and all effect spiritual. We are not living in a physical world but in a spiritual world peopled with spiritual ideas. We are now living in Spirit.

God, or Spirit, governs the universe through great mental laws that work out the divine will and purpose, always operating from Intelligence. This Intelligence is so vast, and the power so great that our human minds cannot even grasp it; all that we can hope to do is to learn something of the *way* in which it works, and by harmonizing ourselves with it, to so align ourselves with Spirit that our lives may be controlled by the great harmony that obtains in all the higher laws of nature, but has been very imperfectly manifested in man. This brings us to the second point of consideration.

Why, and
What Is Man?

WE FIND IN THE PHYSICAL UNIVERSE that automatic laws govern everything; for instance, the tree cannot say, "I will not," because of the law that holds it in place; it grows without any volition of its own. So it is with all nature; but when we come to man we find a different manifestation of the Spirit, a being who can say, "I choose." In all creation, man alone is an individual; man alone is free; and yet man alone wants, is sick, suffers, and is unhappy. "Man marks the earth with ruin"; why? because he has not found his true nature. The very thing that should free him, and eventually will do so, now limits him. God could not make an individual without making him able to think, and he cannot think without bringing upon himself the results of his thought, good or bad. This does not mean using two powers, but using the One from two standpoints. Nothing in itself is either good or bad; all things exist in mind as a potentiality; mind is eternally acting upon thought, continually producing its own images from mind, and casting them out into manifestation. Man must be the outcome of the desire of the Spirit to make something which expresses the same life that It feels. Man is made to be a companion of the Infinite; but to arrive at this exalted plane of being, he must have his freedom, and be let alone to discover his own nature; to return love to his Creator only when he chooses to do so. At the doorway, then, of man's mind this wonderful God has to wait. "Behold, I stand at the door and knock"; the opening must be on the part of the individual.

Man lives in a mind that presses in upon him from all sides with infinite possibilities, with infinite creative power. The divine urge of infinite love crowds itself upon him, and awaits his recognition. Being the image of this Power, *his* thought also must be the Word or cause in the life. At the center of his being is all the power that he will need on the path of his unfoldment; all the mind that man has is as much of this Infinite Mind as he allows to flow through him. We have often thought of God as far off, and of man as a being separate from the All Good; now we are coming to see that God and man are one, and that that One is simply awaiting man's recognition, that he may spring into being and become to man all that he could wish or want. "As the father has inherent life in himself, so hath he given to the Son to have life within himself." It could not be otherwise; we are all in Mind and Mind is always creating for us as we think; and as we are thinking creatures, always thinking, our happiness depends upon our thought. Let us consider the law of our life.

The Law of
Our Lives

*S*PIRIT CREATES THROUGH LAW. The law is always mind in action. Mind cannot act unless intelligence sets it in motion. In the great universal mind man is a center of intelligence, and every time he thinks he sets mind into action. What is the activity of this mind in relation to man's thought? It has to be one of mental correspondence; that is, mind has to reflect whatever thought it casts into it. Wonderful as Universal Mind is, it has no choice but to create whatever thought is given it; if it could contradict that thought, it would not be a unit, since this would be recognizing something outside itself. This is a point in Truth which should not be overlooked. The ONE MIND knows only Its own ability to make whatever is given It; It sees no other power and never analyzes or dissects; It simply KNOWS, and the reason why people do not understand this is that they have not realized what mind is. The ordinary individual thinks of mind only from the limitation of his own environment. The concept he has of mind is the concept of his own thinking, which is very limited.

We are surrounded by an All-Seeing, All-Knowing Mind, which is *One* and runs through all. The belief in the dual mind has destroyed practically all philosophies and religions of the ages, and will continue to do so until the world comes to see that there is but One. Whatever name is given it *there is but One*. It is this One that creates for us, whatever we believe. Our thought operative through this One produces all our affairs. We are all centers in this Mind, *centers of creative thought activity*. There is nothing which appears in the manifest Universe other than an objectified thought, whether it be a bump on your head, a growth on your foot or a planet. It could not be there were it not made out of Mind, for mind is all there is to make anything out of. Whatever is made is made out of it. Nothing exists or can exist without a source from which it springs.

We are not dealing with a negative as well as a positive Power—not two powers but one; a power that sees neither good nor evil, as we see it. It knows only that it is all, and since it is all, it creates whatever is given it. From our limited standpoint we often think of good, and evil; not realizing that, as yet, we do not know the one from the other. What we call good today, we may call evil tomorrow, and what we think to be evil today, we may tomorrow proclaim as the greatest good we have known. Not so with the Great Universal Power of Mind; It sees only Itself, and Its infinite ability to create.

To the thinking person this will mean much; he will

see that he is no longer living in a limited universe, a world of powers, but that he is immersed in an Infinite Creative Medium which, because of Its Nature, has to create for him whatever he believes. Jesus understood this, and in a few simple words, laid down the law of life: "It is done unto all people as they believe." This is a great thing to keep in mind. *It is done unto us;* we do not have to do it, for it is done unto us of a power that knows itself to be all there is. Could we even believe that some material mountain would be moved, the power is there to do it. Without this belief there is no real impulse for the Creative Mind, and we do not get an affirmative answer. We must realize more clearly that this Great Power has to operate through us.

Man's Part

$\mathcal{C}$REATIVE MIND CANNOT FORCE ITSELF upon us because we have the power of self-choice. It recognizes us when we recognize it. When we think that we are limited or have not been heard, it must take that thought and bring it into manifestation for us.

When we look about us and see nature so beautiful, so lavish and so limitless, when we realize that something, some power, is behind all, and sees to it that plenty obtains everywhere, so that in all things manifest there is more than could be used; and when on the other hand we see man so limited, sick, sad and needy, we are disposed to ask this question: "Is God good after all? Does He really care for the people of His creation? Why am I sick? Why am I poor?" Little do we realize that the answer is in our own mouths, in the creative power of our own thought. The average person when told the Truth will still seek some other way.

God has already done for us—in a mechanical way— all that He can do; and having been given the ability, we will have to do for ourselves the rest. Yet the Great Power is always near, ready at any time to help, but we must use it according to its own nature in harmony with its laws. Man should learn that he himself is the center of this Divine activity. Realizing this, he must seek more and more to utilize his own Divine nature, and by so doing he will come more fully under the protection of the great laws that govern all life, manifest and unmanifest. Whatever man is, he must find that because he is made out of God, he must be of the same nature. This Infinite One cannot know anything outside of itself; anything that would be a contradiction of its Divine nature; man's ignorance of his real nature binds him with his own freedom, until he comes to see things as they really are, and not as they appear to be.

In the Infinity of mind, which is the principle of all metaphysics and of all life, there is nothing but mind, and that which mind does. That is all there is in the Universe. That is all there ever was or ever will be. This mind is acted upon by our thought, and so our thought becomes the law of our lives. It is just as much a law in our individual lives as God's thought is in the larger life of the Universe.

For the sake of clearness, think of yourself as in this Mind, think of yourself as a center in it. That is your principle. You think, and Mind produces the thing. One of the big points to remember is that we do not have to create; all that we have to do is to think. Mind, the only Mind that there is, creates.

Few people seem to understand the nature of the law and so think that they have got to do something, even if it is only holding a thought; thinking or knowing is what does the thing. It will make it much easier for us when we realize that we do not have to make anything, just to know; that there is something back of the knowing which does the work for us.

That person gets the best results who realizes that he can use this divine principle; he who can get the clearest concept of his idea, and who can rely on mind to do for him, keeping everything out of his thought that would contradict the supremacy of Spirit or Mind.

By simply holding a thought we could not make anything but by *knowing* in mind what cannot we do?

Bondage
and Freedom

*N*EVER GET AWAY FROM THE FACT that you are surrounded by such a power; it is the principle of demonstration. It knows every thought. As we send forth our thought into it, it does unto us. The person who is ignorant of this law must by that ignorance be bound by his thought, by his human beliefs. One who understands will begin to break these ties that bind him; one by one be will destroy every negative thought until at last he is able to think what he wants to think; and so he frees himself by the use of the same power that at one time bound him. We must destroy all thought that we would not see manifest and hold to that which we would see, until we receive the affirmative answer.

Never struggle, Mind makes things out of Itself, there is no effort made. Don't think that there is so much to be overcome. Have only a calm sense of perfect peace as you realize that God is all, and that you are using the perfect law and that nothing can hinder it from working for you. Many people are learning to do this, and no one has yet failed to demonstrate who has been steadfast, using the law in a consistent and persistent trust.

All that we have to do is to provide the right mental and spiritual attitude of mind and then believe that we already have, and the reward will be with us. We shall see it.

The time will come when we will not have to demonstrate at all because we will be always living so near to the law that it will do all for us without much conscious thought on our part.

So when you say, "I am poor, sick or weak; I am not one with the Creative Mind," you are using that creative power to keep yourself away from the Infinite; and just as soon as you declare that you are one with God, there is a rushing out to meet you, as the Father rushed out to meet the prodigal son. "The Spirit seeketh," but as long as your mind thinks in the terms of conditions you cannot overcome. The difficulty comes from our inability to see our own Divine nature, and its relation to the Universe. Until we awake to the fact that we are one in nature with God, we will not find the way of life; until we realize that our own word has the power of life we will not see the way of life; and this brings us to the consideration of the use of the Word in our lives.

The Word

"THE WORD WAS WITH GOD and the Word was God." "The Word is nigh thee, even in thy own mouth that thou shouldst know it and do it." What does this mean? It clearly states that whatever power there is in the Word (and it says it is All Power) is also in our own mouths. There is no avoiding the fact that the Bible claims for man the same power in his own life and his own world that it claims for God. In the lives of the majority, men do not realize that the Word is in their own mouths. What Word? Little do we realize that this Word which they are so earnestly seeking is every word they hear, think or speak. Do we who are endeavoring to realize the greater truths of life always govern our words? If any word has power, it follows that *all* words have power. It is not in the few moments of spiritual meditation that we demonstrate, but we bring out the possibilities of the hidden word when we are allowing our thoughts to run in any direction; not in the short time spent in silence, but in the long hours stretching themselves into days, months, and years, are we always using the word. An

hour a day spent in silent meditation will not save us
from the confusion of life; the fifty-one percent of a
man's thinking is what counts. It is easy when we are
alone to brave the storms of life; surrounded by our own
exalted atmosphere we feel the strength of the Infinite;
we rise in Spirit, we think we are experiencing the ultimate of truth, that all things are ours. These moments in
a busy life are well spent, but must unavoidably be brief.
But what of the rest of the day; what of the busy street,
of the market place, and of all the daily contact with life?
Do we then obtain? Do we keep on in the same even
way? Or do we fall before the outer confusion of our surroundings? We are still creating the word and setting it
afloat in the great others of life. Are these words creating
for us? *Yes*!

How necessary, then, to "keep the independence of
the solitude"; how seldom we do this!

> "God sent an angel to speak to me—
>   A word He was fain I hear;
>   And the angel brought the message
>   And whispered it in my ear.

> "God knew I needed the word He sent—
>   I had lost the zest of fight;
>   And the right was all but beaten;
>   The wrong it was all but right.

"Simple the word that He sent me—
But it soothed a spirit raw
With the pain of too much striving—
'Twas 'Love fulfills the law.'"

Few people indeed in the day in which we live are well poised. Where do we find the man who can live above his surroundings, who in his own thought can dominate all conditions, and in the midst of the crowd keep his own even way, and his own counsel? When we do meet with such a person we will know him; for we shall find on his face the image of perfect peace.

We shall detect in his bearing the ease and independence that comes only to the man who has found himself and who is centered not in the outer but in the inner world.

Such a character as this has the power to attract to himself all of the best in the world; he is a center toward which all else must gravitate. The atmosphere which he creates and with which he surrounds himself is one of absolute calm and peace. The world at once sees in this man a master, and gladly sits at his feet. And yet this man who has risen above the thought of the world cares not that other people should sit at his feet. He knows that what he has done all may do, and he well knows that all the *teaching* in the world will not produce another such as he. He knows that it is not from the teaching but from the *being* that true greatness springs. So this man does not go around teaching or preaching; he simply IS.

The Man
Who Has Arrived

THE MAN WHO HAS ARRIVED will realize that he has done so in the midst of an outer confusion; he will be the one who has gone into the silence for strength; and has come out into the world equipped with power from on high; but that light which he has received must be kept burning.

Not alone in the silence but in the busy throng must all of us find the way of life. Our every thought creates. For the majority of us these thoughts come in everyday affairs, some of which are very trivia!, but these too will be demonstrated.

We have missed the whole point, unless we have learned so to control our thought that time and place make no difference.

The Power
We Have Within Us

W E HAVE WITHIN US A POWER that is greater than anything that we shall ever contact in the outer, a power that can overcome every obstacle in our life and set us safe, satisfied and at peace, healed and prosperous, in a new light, and in a new life.

Mind, all Mind is right here. It is God's Mind, God's creative Power, God's creative Life. We have as much of this Power to use in our daily life as we can believe in and embody.

The store house of nature is filled with infinite good awaiting the touch of our awakened thought to spring forth into manifestation in our life; but the awakening must be on our part and not on the side of life. We stand at the gateway of limitless opportunity in the eternal and changeless NOW. Now is the day in which to begin the new life that is to lift us up to the greater expression of all that is wonderful. The word that we speak is the Law of our life and nothing hinders but ourselves. We have through ignorance of our real nature misused the power of our word, and behold what it has brought upon us, "the very thing that we feared." But now it shall produce a new thing, a new heaven and a new earth.

Individual
Ideas

*W*E FIND THAT IN THE UNIVERSE every separate idea has a word, a mental concept behind it, and as long as that word remains the thing is held in place in the visible world; when the concept is withdrawn the idea in the visible melts away, disappears; it ceases to vibrate to the word, which is the law behind it, for when the word is withdrawn the condensation of the ether that forms the word melts again into the formless. There was a time when the world was without form, and from the word alone all things were made that are made. When our word says that there is no longer life in our bodies, the life principle withdraws and our bodies return to the substance from which they came. Here is the great mystery of life, that we are able to use this creative word for whatever purpose we may desire, and that word becomes the Law unto the thing for which it was spoken.

And so in our lives we might say that without our word was not anything made that was made. For we are given the power to sit in the midst of our lives and direct all their activities. There is no struggle and no strife necessary. All that we have to do is to know. We must awake and with the glorified consciousness of an emancipated soul use our God-given power.

The Reason for the Universe

THIS UNIVERSE IS THE REASON, first of an Infinite Intelligence which speaks or thinks, and as this thought becomes active within itself, it creates from itself, at the power of its own word, the visible Universe. We are living in a Universal activity of mental law, we are surrounded by a Mind which receives every impression of our thought and returns to us just what we think. Every man, then, is living in a world made for him from the activity of his thought.

It is a self-evident proposition that Mind must create out of Itself; and this Self being Limitless, it follows that its creative power is without limit.

Mind in Action

*E*VERYTHING THAT WE SEE IS the result of mind in action. We all have a body and we have what is called a physical environment; we could have neither if it were not for mind. The law implanted within us is, that we need nothing except ourselves and this All-Wise Creative Mind to make anything; and that just so far as we depend upon any condition, past, present or future, or upon any individual, we are creating chaos, because we are dealing with conditions and not with causes. Every living soul is a law unto himself, but of this great truth few people are conscious. It seems difficult for the race, which feels itself to be so limited, to comprehend the fact that there is a power that makes things directly out of itself, by simply becoming the thing that it makes, and that it does this by self knowing. But we will not demonstrate until we see at least some of this, the greatest truth about life.

We should realize that we are dealing with the principle that is scientifically correct. It will never fail us at any time but is eternally present. We can approach the Infinite Mind with a depth of thought and understanding, knowing that it will respond, knowing that we are dealing with reality.

Jesus, who saw this very clearly, laid down the whole law of life in a few simple words: "It is done unto you as you believe." We do not have to do it, it is done unto us, it is done by a power that is all. Could we believe that a material mountain would be moved, it would be done unto us. But unless we do believe there is no impulse for the creative power and we do not receive. Life externalizes at the level of our thought.

Action and
Reaction

THERE IS SOMETHING THAT CASTS back at us every thought that we think. "Vengeance is mine, I will repay, saith the Lord," is a statement of eternal truth and correspondences against which nothing can stand, and whatever man sets in motion in mind will be returned to him, even as he has conceived within himself and brought forth into manifestation. If we wish to transcend old thoughts we must rise above them and think higher things. We are dealing with the law of cause and effect and it is absolute; it receives the slightest as well as the greatest thought and at once begins to act upon it. And sometimes even when we know this we are surprised at the rapidity with which it works. If we have been misusing this law we need not fail; all that we have to do is to turn from the old way and begin in the new. We will soon work up out of the old law into the new which is being established for us. When we desire only the good the evil slips from us and returns no more.

Arriving at a High Consciousness

THE BEST WAY TO ARRIVE AT THE highest consciousness is to have a great faith in the willingness and
the ability of Life to do all for us, by working through us.
We must believe in the inherent goodness and all-power-
fulness of the Spirit of Truth. And so every path leads us
back to the one point and we must learn to realize the
near presence, the great reality. There, through the door
of our own thought, we enter into the Universal Consciousness, into a complete realization of life and truth,
of love and beauty; and as we sit in the silence of our own
souls and listen, it will be the greatest thing that we will
ever do. In that completeness we are lost and yet we are
found. This is what is meant that a man must lose his
life in order to find it. We are lost to the human and
found in the divine. We realize that we are One with
Cause.

Outer
Suggestions

NEARLY ALL PEOPLE ARE CONTROLLED by outer suggestions, and not by inner realizations. Ordinarily man thinks only what he sees others do, and hears others say. We must all learn so to control the inner life that outside things do not make an impression upon our mentalities. As we are thinking beings, and cannot help thinking, we cannot avoid making things happen to us, and what we need to do is so to control our thought processes that our thinking will not depart from the realization of that which is perfect.

Man is governed by a mind which casts back to him every thought he thinks; he cannot escape from this and need not try; it would be useless. The laws of mind are simple and easy to understand. The trouble with us has been that we have laid down great obstructions, and then have tried to overcome them. Stop trying, stop struggling, begin to be calm, to trust in the higher laws of life, even though you do not see them; they are still there.

Did you ever see the law that causes a plant to grow? Of course you did not, and yet you believe in this hidden law of growth. Why do you believe? Simply because every year, out of the seed time comes a harvest. Shall we not have as great faith in the higher laws of being? To those souls who have dared to believe has come as definite an answer as came to those who believed in receiving a harvest from the planted seed. This law is, and if we would see results we must use it; that is, we must provide the mental receptivity that will prepare us to accept the gift when the Spirit makes it. This receiving is a mental process, a process in which we lose all sense of limitation.

If you wish to demonstrate prosperity, begin to think and talk about it, and to see it everywhere. Do nothing that contradicts this thought either mentally or physically. The world is full of good; take it and forget all else. Rise above depression and be glad that you are saved from adversity; the human mind needs to be cleansed from the morbid thoughts that bind through its false beliefs.

No living soul can demonstrate two things at the same time, if one contradicts the other. There is no way except to let go of all that you *do not wish* to come into your experience, and, in mind, take all that you *do wish*.

SEE, HEAR; TALK ABOUT AND READ ONLY WHAT YOU WISH, AND NEVER AGAIN LET A NEGATIVE THOUGHT COME INTO YOUR MIND.

God knows good only, and when we are in line with good He knows us; when we are out of harmony with good, we say, "God has forgotten us." On the one hand we have an Infinite Intelligence which has brought us up to where we are today; and having done all that it can for us now lets us alone to discover our own nature. On the other hand we have the Infinite Law—which is an activity of God—and we can use it for what we will, only with this provision, that, in so far as we use it for the good of all, are we protected.

The law obtains through all nature that as a man sows, so must he reap. Now the Father has brought us to where we can understand life, and we must go as we choose. If we are in harmony with the great forward movement of the Spirit, there is nothing that can hinder our advancement; if we oppose it, somewhere along our pathway it will crush us. As with individuals so with nations; in so far as they work with a right spirit they prosper; when they begin to fail in the use of this law they begin to fall. He who understands will take the position of one who wishes to work in union with the Power of Good; and to such an one will come all the power that he can conceive of and believe in; his word becomes in expression as the very word of God, and he must realize it to be all powerful. So the one who is truly united with Good will wish to express only the truth for all; and in doing so he is working along the lines of the unfoldment of the Spirit, and though he may seem to fail, from the ordinary standpoint, yet his success is assured; for he is at one with the only ultimate power before which, in time, all else must fall.

The Use of the Greater Consciousness

*I*N PRACTICE THE EMANCIPATED SOUL must always realize that he is in union with the Father; what the Father does, he can do in his own life; what God is, he can become. His word must be spoken with absolute authority; he must *know;* there should be no uncertainty. The word is the only power; everything must come from it, and nothing can stand against it; it is the great weapon which he is to use against all evil and for all good. It is his shield against all adversity and his sure defense against all seeming limitation.

The secret place of the Most High is in his own soul, where God dwells in eternal peace and infinite calm. Here he walks the waters of life undisturbed by the waves and the storm. Divine companionship is his for all eternity. Peace which transcends all human confusion comes, and he realizes that indeed he is honored of the Father. His word is flung out and will work and none can hinder it; the sense of sureness is complete. Heaven and earth may pass away, but the word goes on and on accomplishing that thing for which it was sent; and all power is given to it on earth and in heaven. If he speaks to the sick and they receive; it will heal them. If he says the word of prosperity it will manifest, and nothing can hinder it; the world will abound with good, and his cup run over with life.

What more can we ask! What greater realization of life than to know that God is with us! From this great realization comes peace, a peace which the world little understands, and a calm which is as deep as the infinite sea of love in which he realizes himself to be immersed. Peace brings poise, and the union of these two gives birth to Power. No person can hope to arrive while he believes in two powers; only as we rise to the realization of the One in and through all can we attain. When we speak the word there must be no confusion but only that calm reliance which knows that "Beside me there is none other." Realize that Spirit is All Causation, and that all things are made out of it, by the operation of the word through it, and that you can speak the word that is one with the Spirit and there will be no more confusion. "As the Father has inherent life in himself, so has he given to the Son to have inherent life within himself." "Speak the word only and it shall be done." "The word is in your own mouth that ye should know it and do it." "Stranger on earth, thy home is heaven; Pilgrim, thou art the guest of God."

The Greater Consciousness

*M*AN IS SURROUNDED BY A GREAT universal thought power which returns to him always just as he thinks. So plastic, so receptive is this mind, that it takes the slightest impression and molds it into conditions. There are two things in man which his thought affects, his body and his environment. At all times he is given absolute control over these two things, and from the effect of his thought upon them he cannot hope to escape.

At first, being ignorant of this fact, he binds himself by a misuse of the laws of his being; but as he begins to see that he himself is responsible for all that comes to him on the path of life, he begins to control his thought, which in its turn acts on the universal substance to create for him a new world.

The great soul is learning more and more to dare to fling out into mind a divine idea of himself, and to see himself perfect and whole.

If he has a divine thought he will get a divine thing, if he has a human thought he will get a human thing; he will receive whatever his innermost thought embodies.

And so we find in the Bible twice repeated these words: "To the pure Thou wilt show Thyself pure and to the froward Thou wilt show Thyself froward." It is done unto all as they believe.

We often wonder why it is that we are not making better demonstrations. We look about and observe that some are getting wonderful results, they are speaking the word and people are being healed. We see others struggling along with the word, and nothing seems to happen; and when we inquire into the reason for all this we find it to be very plain indeed. All is mind and we are mental, we are in mind and can only get from it what we first think into it. We must not only think but we must know. We have to provide within ourselves a mental and spiritual likeness for the thing desired. The reason why so few succeed, then, must be because they have not mentally really believed to the exclusion of all that would deny the thing which they believe in. And the reason why others do succeed must also be because they have absolutely believed and allowed real power to flow through and out into expression. They must have a real concept of life. Hold an object in front of a mirror and it will image in the mirror the exact size of the object. Hold a thought in mind and it will image in matter the exact likeness of the thought. Let us take this image which we hold before a mirror and change it ever so slightly and there will be a corresponding change in the reflection. It is just the same in the mental world; *whatever is imaged is brought forth* from mind into manifestation.

We must not deny that which we affirm. We must reason only from that cause which is spiritual and mental and weed out all thought that would deny its power in our lives. There seems to be something in the race thought that says man is poor; man is limited; that there is a lack of opportunity; that times are hard; that prices are high; that nobody wants what I have to offer. No person succeeds who speaks these ideas. When we express ourselves in this way we are using a destructive power. All such thoughts must go, and we must all realize that we are an active center in the only power there is.

We must get the perfect vision, the perfect conception; we must enlarge our thought until it realizes all good, and then we must swing right out and use this Almighty Power for definite purposes. We should daily feel a deeper union with Life, a greater sense of that indwelling God, the God of the everywhere, within us. When we speak into this Mind we have sown the seed of thought in the Absolute and may rest in peace. We do not have to make haste, because it is done unto all as they believe. "In that day that they shall call upon me I will answer."

People will often ask, "What is the best method for demonstration?" There is but one answer to that question; the Word is the only possible method of demonstrating anything; the word really felt and embodied in our thought. Then the word becomes flesh and dwells among us and we behold and experience it. We will ask for no other way when we understand this.

The person who does not understand these laws will be likely to say that this is presumptuous; that it is even sacrilegious; but this comes only from a lack of understanding of the fact that all is governed by law, and that all law is impersonal and universal. We have just as much right to use spiritual law as to use so-called physical laws. Strictly speaking there is no such a thing as a physical law, as all things are spiritual and all law is a law of the activity of the Spirit. The greatest use of these laws will always come to that soul who is the most deeply spiritual, as such an one comes the nearest to using law as God uses it. So to the really great soul there must come a very close relationship with the Invisible God; this relationship cannot be expressed in words but only in inner feeling which transcends the power of words to express. God must become the great reality, not simply as the principle of life, but more as the great Mind which knows, and which at all times understands and responds. To say that God does not understand our desires would be to rob the divine mind of all consciousness and place God lower in the scale of being than we ourselves are. On the other hand we must be careful not to believe that God thinks evil and understands that which is not perfect, as then we would have an imperfect being for the First Cause.

We should more and more learn to think of things in the absolute, that is, to think of things as not limited by conditions. Realize at all times that the Spirit makes things out of Itself, and needs no beginning except its own self-recognition. Then we must cognize our relation to this great power as one of absolute correspondence; what we think into it, it takes up and does for us as we think. It should not be an effort so to think; we should do so with ease, without strain. The law must return to us; we have no responsibility except to provide the proper channel. It can return only in the exact way that we think. If we think struggle is the reality, we shall gain our demonstration, but struggle will have to be the result. There is a law of reflection between Mind and the one who thinks; and it is not only what a man thinks but also how he thinks that "shall be done unto him."

If you believe absolutely that you can do a certain thing, the way will always be opened for you to do it; if also you believe that time will have to elapse, then you are making that a law, and time will have to elapse. If on the other hand you believe that mind knows just how and never makes mistakes, but lets it be done unto you, then it will be done. Confusion brings more confusion; peace begets more peace; we cannot imagine the Great Spirit hurrying or worrying, fretting or trying to make anything happen. The only reason we worry and fret is because we have thought there was some other power which could bring confusion. Such is not the case. There is but *one,* and we are always using that one but using it according to our belief. This is our divine birthright, nothing hinders but ourselves. Remember that since all is mind, you cannot demonstrate beyond your ability to comprehend

mentally, that is, beyond your ability to *know* about a
certain thing. For instance, suppose you wish to heal
someone who is sick; your ability to do this will depend
entirely upon your ability to see perfection mentally, coupled also with the realization that your word destroys
everything unlike itself. If you try to see perfection *for a
few minutes only,* it will never heal. Your thought goes on
at all times, and in the moments when you least realize
it, conditions are being molded for you. It is not enough
to declare consciously for the truth. The truth must be
lived or no good results will be forthcoming.

The Perfect
Universe

*T*HE ONE WHO DESIRES TO HEAL must stop seeing, reading about, discussing, or listening to conversation about sickness. There is no other way under the sun except as we let go of that which we do not desire, and take that which we wish to have. There is too much of this deceiving ourselves into thinking that we can do two ways at once. We may deceive ourselves and possibly other people, but the law remains the same, a Law of mental correspondences, and nothing else. We cannot go beyond our ability to realize the truth; water rises only to its own level. In our patients as well as in ourselves and our environment we will reflect what we are, not at our best in the few moments of silence, but in the long run of ordinary life and thought.

To acquire the larger consciousness is no easy task. All that we have believed in which contradicts the perfect whole must be dropped from our thought, and we must come to realize that we are now living in a perfect universe, peopled with perfect spiritual beings, each of which (coupled with the Great Divinity) is complete within

himself. We must see that we are one in the great *one*,
and then we will not separate or divide, but unite and add
to, until in time we will find that we are living in an entirely different world from that in which we had once
thought we were living. Of course, this will meet with
much opposition from those unenlightened souls whom
we must contact in the world. But what of that? Remember, the great man is the one who can keep in the crowd
the calm, even thought, the deep, divine reliance on principle. And more, this is the only way to help or to save
the world. In time all people will come to the same understanding. You are lifting up the standard of life, and
those who are ready will follow. You have no responsibility to save the world except by exemplifying the truth. The
world must save itself.

All are alike; there is no difference between one person and another. Come to see all as a divine idea; stop all
negative thought; think only about what you want, and
never about what you do not want, as that would cause a
false creation. Too much cannot be said about the fact
that all are dealing with only one power, making and un-
making for man through the creative power of his own
thought. If there is something in your life that you do
not want there, stop fighting it—forget it!

About Struggle–
Karma

*T*HERE IS TOO MUCH STRUGGLE coming into the metaphysical thought. Often we hear some seeker after truth say, "I have a big fight ahead." O foolish and untaught, how can you hope to enter in? The kingdom comes not from without, but from within, *always*. Stop all struggle and wait upon the sure principle that creates whatever it wills because there is nothing to oppose it. As long as we think that opposition exists we are blocking the way for the clearer vision. Those that take up the sword must perish by it; not because God is a jealous God, but because that is the way the law must work.

Cause and effect must obtain everywhere. Do not even fuss about your Karma; too often we hear people say, "This is my Karma." This may be true enough, but how many people know what they mean when they use the word Karma? Do you realize that your Karma is nothing but your false thinking, and that the only way to escape it is to think the truth, and that brings in the higher law? When the greater comes in the lesser leaves because there is no longer anything to give life to it.

The past is gone when we learn to forgive and to forget.

This erases from mind all that is held against us, and even our sins "Are remembered no more against us forever." Fate is in our own hands, and when we will rise to that pure atmosphere where we see things in their completeness, and know that an All-Wise Power is behind it all, we will see that the Infinite Mind could wish for us only that which expresses itself in limitless terms. The whole trouble has been that we reason as men and not as *Gods*. "I say ye are *Gods* and every one of you Sons of the Most High."

The great law of life is thinking and becoming; and when we think from the lofty heights of the Spirit we will become great, and not until then. Do not try to convince any one of the truth; that will bring confusion. Truth is, just as much as God is; and the whole world is coming gradually into the realization of it. Keep the truth within your own soul, lift your own self above the confusion of life, and then people will believe. So all our thought is to be created in the realization of the One becoming the many, without struggle, without fear; stripped of all that denies the truth.

How limited we are, how little our thought! How the human race rises in the morning, plods off to the day's work, plods home at night, sore and tired, eats and sleeps, works and dies. As has been said of man, "Man works hard to get money to buy food to get strength to work hard to get money to buy food to get strength to work hard to get money, etc." This was never intended; it is the curse imposed on the man who believed in two powers, one of good and one of evil. To us there has come a greater vision, and to those who believe and act as though it were true it is proving itself.

We must turn from all human thought and experience. We are not down trodden, depraved and miserable sinners, born in sin and conceived in iniquity and shame, some to go to heaven and some to hell and all to the eternal glory of God. This is a lie, it always was and always will be. But as long as we believe in a lie it seems to be present with us.

Man is born of the Spirit of God Almighty, is pure, holy, perfect, complete and undefiled; is at one with his eternal principle of being. Many people are finding this out and as a monument to its truth millions are daily proving it for themselves.

Somewhere down the path of human experience we will all awake to the realization that we ourselves are heaven or hell.

We live in Spirit awaiting the touch of thought that believes. All people look, a few see.

Part Two

Practice

Introductory

HE ONE WHO WISHES TO PRACTICE metaphysics must first, last, and all the time realize that he himself is a center of the divine activity; he must know that whatever God is in the Universal, he is in the world in which he lives. He must know that all things are made out of Spirit, which is First Cause; nothing comes before Spirit. Operating upon itself out of itself, it makes what it will out of its own perfect desire. He must think of the Spirit as the Father of his own life, eternally bound to him, eternally binding him to it.

He must know that the Spirit not only can manifest through him, but that it wishes to do so; "The Father seeks such to worship Him." The practitioner who understands the truth knows that as long as God exists, he will exist; that he could no more become non-existent than God could. Walking, talking, moving in God, he must not only see the Divine Being as the great unknown Cause, but he must go a step further and see God as the great self-knowing, understanding power of Infinite Intelligence, thinking through his own thought and willing into his own life all power and all good. More than this, God must become within his own soul the greater self, the inner life, the inner light that is to light his path with sure step to the attainment of the greater ideals. God is to become the great friend of his life, understanding him, and helping him at all times to understand all things.

No more books, no more teachers, no more preachers, creeds or candlesticks will he ever need. The old methods must vanish into their native nothingness, as the great realization that God is all in his life dawns upon his awakened thought.

"Naught is the squire, when the king's at hand;
    Withdraw the stars, when dawns the sun's brave
        light."

He must know that not height, nor depth, nor any other thing, can come between the soul and its perfect Creator. Too long have we listened to people; now our own soul shall speak in a language that is unmistakable; now shall we ourselves become masters of all life and interpreters of all mysteries. Now my Father and I are one.

As the word of God goes forth and sets in motion the all law, so must we realize because we are one with the word that our own thought has the power of expression. The one who wishes to heal must come to see all evil as impersonal, fastening it to no one, but realizing that it is simply false thought; the healer knows that the word which he is to speak will destroy this false impression; and by erasing it, it will vanish.

There should be absolutely no sense of responsibility beyond speaking the word in positive faith, knowing. All struggle belongs to the Old Order; in the New peace takes the place of confusion, faith answers the cry of doubt and fear, and the Word is supreme.

We must know that our word is law, and cannot be set aside by the false thought of the world. Every time that we state a truth, we must know that that truth destroys all that is unlike itself and frees the thought of the one whom we wish to help and to heal.

This word must become the new Law which frees. People are sick because they think sickness and will be healed only when they turn from this kind of thought and begin to think in terms of health.

The Same Power
Used in Two Ways

*T*HERE IS ONLY ONE POWER, but we use it in two ways, either to destroy or to save. The blessing and the curse are one and the same thing; the power of mind used either affirmatively or negatively; the word used in fear and doubt or in faith and assurance.

You do not have to understand material philosophy or be learned in the books of the human race. All these things may be good in their place, but to one who understands the greater laws of life they are as simple babblings—

> "An infant crying in the night,
> An infant crying for the light.
> And with no language but a cry."

We no longer cry, we Know. We no longer ask if there be a God, or if we dare to speak to Him lest we die; we do not analyze, dissect, affirm, or deny, *We know.*

We trust our own word because first we "Know in whom we have believed." The sooner the one who is striving to attain will realize that truth must become revealed through his own soul, and not that of another, the sooner he will attain. We must then become immune from the race suggestion of an hypnotic power that sets itself up as an authority. There is no other authority than your own soul, as "There is no law but that your soul has set." Leave authorities to smaller minds, and to those who need a leader because of this their own self-confessed weakness, and be *Free*. Dare to "*Stand* amidst the eternal way" and proclaim your own *Atonement* with all the power that there is, was, or ever will be.

Practically the whole human race is hypnotized, thinking whatever it is told to think. We get our concepts from our physical environment, we say, "See sin, sickness and death, misery, unhappiness and calamity." And this concept we are giving to the creative, impersonal Mind, and so we are making a law for ourselves that will produce what we believe in. Do we really know what law means? *It means that which will exact the utmost farthing from our thought.*

Like produces like, attracts like, creates like. If we could see our thought and take a picture of it and of our conditions we would see no difference between the two, for they are really but the inside and the outside of the same thing.

We cannot make affirmations for fifteen minutes a day and spend the rest of our time denying the thing which we have affirmed, and affirming the thing which we have denied, and obtain the results which we seek. We send out the word and it sets the power in motion; then we think the opposite thing which neutralizes the first word, and zero is the result.

We cannot demonstrate one iota beyond our mental ability to conceive and steadfastly to embody. Infinite as Creative Power is, receptive and quick as it is, it can only become to us what we first think into it. God can do *for* us only what He can do *through* us.

Dare to say, "Behold I am he. Great men have come and gone, and behold a greater now stands here where I stand, and I am that one." The world will laugh and perhaps scorn. The Christian world will hold up its hands in holy horror, lest you blaspheme; the unchristian world will smile knowingly. Neither the one nor the other will understand, but the understanding of either counts for nothing. You are now free, and your freedom will yet save the world from itself. The great soul finds within himself the Divine companionship which he needs. He finds within himself the "Peace which passeth all understanding" and the power to do all things. *All Power!* He speaks, his word is Law and it is done unto him of all the power there is. His word knows itself to be the law of life unto all for whom it is spoken and who receive it.

Healing the Sick

WE SHALL BE CALLED UPON TO heal all manner of disease, to comfort the sorrowing and to bring peace to the distressed. First we must heal ourselves. When we are healing others we are also healing ourselves. A healer's work takes place within himself. This idea of "sending out thought" and "holding thought" is all a mistake. Things come into being not only by "taking thought" but *by knowing that the Word is infinite.* This word is in your own mouth, and there alone can it be spoken. Here your responsibility begins and here it ends, *in your own mouth.* You must feel no responsibility for the recovery of your patient, for it brings confusion and disturbance to be always wondering if it is working. It must work, if you have the sure faith, and your patient is receptive. You are dealing with the same power that said, "Let there be light" and there was light.

If your patient is suffering from a belief that he is dying of some dread disease, you must know that when you speak the word it will destroy this false belief and set him free. There must be no doubt about the power in the word which you speak. It should be said in perfect calm, in peace, and with absolute faith that it will work. This word then establishes the law of life unto the patient, it casts out all fear, it destroys all false sense of a material life and realizes that all is an expression of a perfect God; and so leaves nothing that can sin, be sick, suffer or die. When you are as sure of this as that you breathe, when you truly know within yourself, your patient will be healed, provided he also believes. If he does not believe it is not your fault, and you will have done for him all that can be done.

Denials

SOME PEOPLE TEACH THE USE of denials. This must be settled by each individual for himself. Here and at all times we must settle every question from within and not from without. No living soul can say how another should or should not work. Beware of the danger of a self-appointed authority; this danger is as apt to come into New Thought as it was in the Old. *No one is your authority on anything.* Let us look into the philosophy of denials. We find that many people teach and practice them, and we do not wish in any way to criticize them. Their reasoning is this: "All disease is an image of thought held in mind until it appears in the body." It is true that without the ability to think man could not be sick. If he thinks a sick thought it will make him sick; when he changes his thought and thinks health, he is healed. It is taught that since sickness is negative thought, it must be counteracted by a positive thought, and that the best way is to deny the sick and affirm the positive thought; for instance, "There is no matter, and nothing can be the matter. This man has no material stomach, he is spiritual and not material; his lungs are not made of matter, they are spiritual ideas; I deny that man can be sick or suffer or die." All this may be accurate; man is a spiritual idea, and so must be perfect in his real nature; but there is a question if this is the *better* way. When we look into the creative way of the spirit we find it impossible for denial to enter, as the Spirit recognizes no opposite to its own nature.

It knows that *"I Am and beside me there is no other."* The Spirit does not deny anything, it simply affirms itself to be that which it desires to be. Seeing and recognizing no opposite to itself, it finds no need of denial, indeed, this thought need not enter the mind; if we are working with the Spirit we need not deny but state the affirmative attitude of mind, realizing that we are dealing with the only power that exists. There is a subtle danger in using denials; we may deny to such an extent as to erect a barrier or build a mountain to overcome. Once realize that God makes things out of Himself simply by speaking, and you will never again use denials in treating. All that needs changing is the false thought, and by affirming that your word destroys everything but itself you will embody all that a denial could. In those systems that teach denials we find that the more enlightened ones are gradually using the affirmative method, and as this is the growth of experience there can be no doubt that it is the better method. Of one thing we may be sure, the Spirit *never denies. It simply knows that I am.*

The Use of
Affirmations

*T*HE AFFIRMATION IS THE GREAT weapon of the healer; it is in alignment with the way of the original creative spirit and is the true use of the Word of All Power. We need only to say that our word is the law unto the case and calmly state what we want to be done, and then say and do nothing that contradicts it and wait for the fulfillment of that word. There is a power that operates on what we say, and it is done unto us, and we need have no fear about the results.

If I am treating Mary Jones I need only say I am helping her, and go to work within myself to realize that she is *now* a perfect being, made in the image of God. I must know that I am destroying all imperfection; when I know within myself that I am speaking the truth and realize that she is perfect, the healing is done as far as I am concerned. If she receives she is healed; I am not responsible for her receptivity. Know that there is a power that corresponds to your own mental attitude and you will see that the way you are believing is what makes things happen the way they do. Always believe in what you are doing; never see the negative side of life, never talk about it, or listen to talk of other people, and never think about or see imperfection; and you will have no trouble in making demonstrations.

The Highest
Attitude of Mind

THE HIGHEST ATTITUDE OF MIND, from which all else springs, is one of perfect calm and absolute trust in the Spirit. The one who can with perfect confidence look into the future and with perfect ease of mind rest in the present, and who never looks backward, but who has learned to be still in his own soul and wait upon the Spirit, *he* is the one who will the most completely demonstrate the supremacy of spiritual thought over all so-called material resistance. "Be still and know that *I Am God.*"

Non-Resistance

"*R*ESIST NOT EVIL AND IT WILL flee from you." Here is a statement of one of the great laws of our being. When we resist we make a mental image of the thing we are fighting, and that tends to have it created for us. When we learn to look only at what we want and never at what we do not want, we will no longer resist anything. "Suffer it to be so now." You need not try to change the world. Let it alone; all people are doing the best they can. No one needs to be saved but yourself, and the sooner you realize this the sooner you will attain. Get over that "holier than thou" attitude. It is an illusion that many people suffer from, especially in the religious world. The world is all right; it is not going to Hell; it is on the way to Heaven. It is getting good so fast that in the process many things are being overturned and confusion appears to be on the surface. A great change is taking place, and on the surface the results are as yet a little mixed, but underneath, the power is at work destroying all unlike itself. In time all will come to see this. What a load of responsibility we assume that we were never meant to carry.

Remember that in the Divine plan no mistakes are made and that if God could have done it in a better way he would have done it differently. No souls are lost, for all "Live and move and have their being in Him" and "God is not a God of the dead but of the living, for in His sight all are alive." Too long have we believed in the negative simply because we have allowed ourselves to become hypnotized by a few strong-minded people, and by those who have imposed upon the race a mass of false philosophy.

Be Alive

HERE IS NO PLACE IN THE New Order for "dead ones." The true metaphysician is alive to all that is useful. Filling his place in the events of the human race, he takes part in all its labor and in all its fun. Pessimism must be relegated to the scrap heap. There is no place among the living for the dead. "Let the dead bury their dead." "Follow thou me." Do not hesitate to enter into the game of life, but do so with a zest and an enthusiasm that overflows with life. Fill yourself with the radiance of a life running over with power and usefulness. Then shall the world see your light.

People in the New Thought above all others should enter into the business world, into educational vocations, into politics, into every walk of life, and there prove before a waiting world, tired of itself, that a "man's a man," with this difference: not a "son of man" but a "Son of God."

Be Happy

OW CAN WE HOPE TO MAKE the world see the right way unless we overflow with joy? The world has now too many sad faces. We see them everywhere, that resigned look that seems to say, "One rebuff more or less makes no difference; I am already so sad that nothing matters; I can bear it." This was all right when we thought everything was all wrong, but now we know that "all's well with the world" we must get over this depression which robs us of the power of attraction of the good things of life, and "enter in."

The man who is always glad will surround himself with people who are happy, and life will be a continual enjoyment. This robs no one; it does not make a race of irresponsible people; it makes a world of joy, a world that is good to live in.

No one wants to associate with the dead. People are looking for a more abundant expression of life, not for depression and fault-finding. Find fault with no one, and more than this find no fault with yourself. Get over the thought of condemning people and things. People and things are all right; let them alone and enjoy life. Your very atmosphere will cheer and uplift the people who contact you, and a new life will enter into them. Overflow.

"As it's given me to perceive,
I most certainly believe
When a man's glad plumb through,
God's pleased with him same's you."

Live in
the Present

*L*IFE IS FOR US TODAY. There will be no change for tomorrow unless we do the changing today. Today we are setting in motion the power of tomorrow. Today is God's day, and we must extract from it what of life we are to live. Tomorrow in the divine course of events will care for itself. The soul that learns to live in the great gladness of today will never weary of life but will find that he is living in an eternal here and now. Now, all good is his; now, all life, truth and love are his; now, he has entered in, and the good things of life are his today.

"Lord for tomorrow and its needs I do not pray,
Make me to do thy will just for today."

Let your soul sing today and the song that comes tomorrow will be all the sweeter, will ring out over the vistas of time with an unmistakable clearness. Here is a soul who knows himself and has found life within himself, who has met God today. No more waiting, no more longing, no more weary roads to travel. He has arrived. The goal is won and peace has come at last. Today.

See the Good
in All Things

*L*EARN TO SEE GOD IN ALL manifestation, in all people, through all events. The ordinary person sees only the lump of matter. Not so with the awakened soul. He sees in all things the Divine Mind at work molding out into expression what it feels itself to be of life, of color, of form and beauty. There are some illusioned ones who claim that what we see is all false, and that the so-called material universe is an unreality. What a mistake! What we see is the body of God, full, free, complete, whole.

> "A primrose by the river's brim,
> A yellow primrose was to him,
> And it was nothing more."

He never saw the idea behind—it was seen only as matter, matter, matter; yet what he could have seen was God's thought of himself coming out into wonderful beauty, and color, and form; The Infinite One manifesting in an infinite variety of forms. What do you see when you look upon the human form, the crowning glory of God's perfect creation? Matter, matter, matter? Flesh, blood and bones? Indeed, these may be passing into expression, but what of the idea, what of the reality of the body? This body of ours is as real as God is real. It would not be if it were an illusion. The very touch of the flesh should send a thrill through the whole body, bringing up its vibration to a higher pitch, to a finer form. The body is not one "mass of pollution," it is the temple of the *living God* and should be so thought of. Too long have we condemned it, and must free it by reversing the process. Of all things on earth the human body is the most beautiful, the most wonderful and the most God-like.

"If you do not love your brother whom you have seen, how can you love God whom you have not seen?" Human magnetism is not hypnotism, it is the divinity of man in expression; and when we learn to convert human passion into divine love, to transmute the lower into the higher, we shall have with us a power of attraction against which nothing can stand.

"He who hath ears to hear, let him hear."

When we behold a beautiful sunset we should see the wonderful thought of God, the radiance of his presence. In the strength of the hills we should see the strength of the Spirit; and seeing all things as spiritual ideas, we should learn to love them, because God has made them and given them to us to use. The soul who in ecstasy can rush up to a tree and embrace it realizes more of God than all the bigoted priests who have ever lived. The one who can sniff the ocean breeze with delight feels the presence of the Divine Being more keenly than does the one who kneels in despair before an awful God of Justice.

Learn then how to appreciate Nature and Nature's God. Spend much time in the out of doors; look up at the stars; let them be your companions; tread the pathless ways of the trees and the giant forests and see God in everything that you look upon, the God of the everywhere.

Be Expectant

*E*XPECT THE BEST TO HAPPEN. Don't sit around waiting for trouble; have absolutely nothing to do with it. It is no part of the divine plan. It is an illusion of the material sense. One who has learned to trust will not be surprised even when he finds things coming from the most unexpected sources. All things are man's to use and then let go of. What more can we ask? We want nothing that we have to keep; things are to use not to hold. Expect that everything is to come your way. Be content and cheerful if you wish to attract from out the store of the infinite. Open up your whole consciousness to the greater possibilities of life. Line up with the big things. When you speak the word expect it to happen. Know that it must be as you say. This will not be fooling yourself, it will simply be using the law as it is meant to be used.

Expanding
Our Thought

ALL THINGS COME TO US through the use of our
thought. If we have a small concept of life we will
always be doing small things. First in the creative series is
the Word, but the Word carries us no further than our
consciousness back of it. Unless we are constantly ex-
panding our thought we are not growing. Growth is the
law of life and it is necessary. We cannot stand still. If
you want to do a new thing, get a new thought and then
you will have the power of attraction which has the possi-
bility of drawing to you the circumstances which will
make for the fulfillment of your desires. Get over the old
idea of limitation. Overcome all precedents and set yourself in the new order of things. If you want to build a rail-
road, you will never do it unless you get over the idea that
the most you can hope for in life is to sell peanuts. Let
the people sell peanuts for a living who think in the terms
of peanuts. Get out of the rut. God has created you for a
glorious future; dare to fling out into mind the greater
assurances about yourself.

The Power
of a Treatment

A TREATMENT HAS AS MUCH POWER as we put into the word which we speak when we are giving it. This does not mean screwing up our mind or using our will power, or using force from the material standpoint. It means simply knowing that what we say will be done unto us of a Power which can do anything that is given It to do. We must know that our word breaks down every material law and sets the patient free to express God. We must know that the word would endure even though all else should fail. "Heaven and earth will pass away but my word will accomplish." In calm confidence and perfect faith, speak and wait upon the perfect law. Get that mental attitude that never wavers. Be sure and it will be done.

Repeating
the Treatment

ONE TREATMENT WOULD HEAL anything if it were not for the fact that people are constantly receiving false suggestions from the outer life. As it now stands we should treat until we get results, always expecting that it will happen at once. Every treatment should be complete, and at the close we should always realize that it is done.

The word spoken once from the mind that knows is immediately taken up by the Mind in which we live, and this Mind begins to create around the word, which is the seed, the thing thought of. We must speak that word with authority. There can be no wondering if it is going to work. When we plant a seed in the ground and water and care for it, we never doubt but a plant will spring into being. So it is with the word. It is acted upon by some power which we do not see, but that the power is there there is no doubt, since all who go about it get results. As Thomas Edison says of electricity, "It Is; use it;" so we say of mind, "It Is; use it." Always remember that your every thought is the way that you are treating, since it is the way that you are thinking.

Impersonal
Healing

*T*HE VERY PRESENCE OF ONE that understands the truth will have a great power of healing. The reason for this is that we are all in Mind, and we have with us at all times our thought, and since all manifestation is the result of mind in action, and we are thinking beings and are always causing mind to act, the very presence of our thought will have some power to act upon whatever we are thinking about. We are dealing with a power which in itself is limitless. We limit it, and so it cannot become to us the bigger thing. Of itself the power is the same that made the worlds, and it cannot realize any sense of limitation. "They could not enter in because of their unbelief and because they limited the Holy One of Israel." Stop limiting things. Things are as big as we make them, no more, no less. There is room at the top. Get on top of everything, and dare to dominate the earth. All things are given us to use; make use of them. Everything is limitless, and we must see the truth that the fault is not in the Law but in ourselves when we fail. Not with God but with man. *Dare, Dare, Dare.*

81

Think of the bigness of things in the universe, think of the number of grains of sand, the profusion of all life, and never again limit anything. *All is yours to use.* Jesus would never have become the Christ unless he had had the courage to say, "Behold, *I Am He.*" You will never attain until in some degree you are able to say the same thing of yourself.

We must learn to reach out and take what is meant for us, the greater life, the all good. People say, "Yes, but how do you do it?" Simply know that God makes things out of Himself by speaking the word, and that in your own life you can do the same. All people can think, and all people can speak, at least mentally; this is all that you need to begin on. The word is at the center of all creation and is first cause, the starting point of all that you see. The word is in your own mouth, and all that you have to do is to speak it. The trouble is that we are speaking the word, and in the next breath we are denying its power by seeing something that contradicts It. If the word is the way that God creates, it is the right way. If it works for God, shall it not work for us? As yet our word is more or less imperfect; but more and more it will become perfect and so the outer condition will be brought up to the inner word. All words have as much power as we put into them when we speak. "The word is already in our own mouths." That word is all that you will ever need to bring happiness, health and success to you.

Do you wish to live in a perfect world peopled with

friends who love you, surrounded by all that is beautiful and pleasing? Do you wish to have the good things of life? There is but one way and that way is as sure as that the sun shines. Forget all else and think only upon what you want. Control all thought that denies the real, and as the mist disappears before the sun so shall all adversity melt before the shining radiance of your own exalted thought.

The prodigal son remained a prodigal only so long as he chose to do so. When the thought came to him to return he was greeted by the Father with outstretched hands. So shall we find that when we turn to that world which is perfect there will be something that will turn with us, and we shall behold the new heaven and the new earth; not in some far off place somewhere beyond the clouds, but here and now shall we become free.

We must do away with all that hinders the true growth, all the little thoughts that hinder us from becoming. Human strife comes from the thought that there is not enough to go around. Forget it; we cannot use even what we see, and what we do not see is infinite. You will rob no one by becoming prosperous, and the laws that underly this state of being are simple and easy to understand, and not hard to attain for the one who is willing to let go of the negative state of being.

Prosperity

ERE ARE A FEW SIMPLE RULES for prosperity that are as sure of working as that water is sure to be wet. First remember that nothing happens by chance. All is law and all is order. You create your own laws every time you think. There is something, call it what you will, but there is a Power around you that knows and that understands all things.

This Power works like the soil; it receives the seed of your thought and at once begins to operate upon it. It will receive whatever you give to it and will create for you and throw back at you whatever you think into it.

This means that the practitioner should be very careful how he is thinking at all times. Not alone in the moments of the deeper silence are we treating our patients, but perhaps more than this we are treating them in an impersonal way at all times. When we take a patient into our thought for a treatment there will be a constant stream of consciousness flowing out to him, during all the time that he is in our care. We should be very careful of our thoughts as we realize the deep truths of mental action and reaction.

What Is the
Spiritual Mind?

HAT IS TRUE SPIRITUALITY? Many people have asked this and as many have answered it. I do not pretend to know more about this all important topic than others, but to the thinking person who has come to realize that all is love, yet at the same time all is governed by law, there must be a different answer given than the one we ordinarily hear. The average religious person thinks that spirituality must manifest in some unnatural way, such as giving up all personal pleasure and becoming resigned to whatever happens; that we must give up most of what life holds here; that in some far-off future perhaps we may attain. This was not the case with the man Jesus. We have more accounts of his being at feasts and weddings and similar gatherings than at other places. His first miracle was performed at a wedding feast, and we must remember that here he even turned water into wine for the pleasure of the guests of the house. Perhaps we have made a mistake about what true spirituality means.

Other people think we must live some kind of an excluded life in order to obtain. Perhaps this may be true of the weak ones. But what of the world? What of the busy street? Is it not to be saved also? Jesus spent much time with the common people as well as with the rich. And it is certain that he also spent much time alone with the Spirit.

What is the Spirit, anyway? We all answer, "Why, of course, it is God." Where is the Spirit? It is present at all times and in all places. *True spirituality must simply mean coming to realize the presence of this Spirit.* It must be coming to rely upon it more than anything else. The one then who is the most spiritual is simply the one who *relies the most;* that is all. No matter where he is, he must rely, he must trust, he must believe. We do not have to give up anything but negative thought and act. We do not want to do anything that contradicts the forward march of the unfoldment of the Spirit, so all that we think and do must be in line with that which is right. But who shall say what is and what is not right? *Remember this forever, only your own soul shall say what is right and what is wrong.* "To thine own self be true, and it shall follow as the night the day, thou canst not then be false to any man." Look to no one for guidance. This is the "blind leading the blind." The Almighty has put the truth into your own soul; look there and there alone for it. Many people seem to think that for a man to look spiritual he must have no color in his face, have some kind of far-away truth; he must be peculiar either in looks, or in the way he dresses.

To one who knows the truth, both praise and blame sound alike, but from the human standpoint at least a person cannot help being amused at the way in which the world judges true spirituality. My idea of true spirituality is that a man should live a perfectly normal life, entering into and enjoying all in life that is clean and good. He should place himself absolutely under the divine guidance. Other than this he will seem just like other people, neither better nor worse. Get over all kinds of unnatural thought and remember that all is good. Neither criticize nor condemn people or things. You are spiritual in so far as you trust in the Spirit, at all times, in all places, under all conditions. In order to do this you do not have to seclude yourself from the world. To do so is an open confession of your own weakness and lack. There are moments when it is best to be alone with the Power. From these moments we gather strength. To keep that strength to ourselves is pure selfishness. Walk, talk, live with the human race, hand in hand with all people and unified with all events, live and love and learn. Be natural and normal. If you seek to enter some other way it must all be done over again, for no one lives or dies unto himself but unto all people.

The Church
of God

THE CHURCH OF GOD IS NOT built with hands, it is eternal in the heavens; it is not lighted with candles; its dome is heaven and it is lighted by the stars of God's illumined thought, and each member in his separate star "shall draw the thing as he sees it, for the God of things as they are." Here all people recognize the God within their own souls and ask for and see no other God. When you can look upon all Creation as the perfect work of a perfect God, you will become a member of this church. I doubt very much if the church universal admits members from the church individual. When you can see in the saint and the sinner one and the same person, when you can realize that the one who kneels before the altar and the one who lies drunk in the street is the same one, when you can love the one as much as you do the other, no doubt you will be able to qualify. As it now is we have too many preachers who do not understand, that have no purpose; too many prayers, too many creeds, too many teachers, that have no message; too many churches, too many "learned" people, and too few *thinkers*. "The Kingdom of Heaven cometh not by observation." It is the "Still, small voice" within the soul that speaks. The expanded thought will never wish to join or be joined to. Nothing human can contain it. It feels the limitation of form and ceremony and longs for the freedom of the Spirit, the great out of doors, the Great God of the everywhere. Alone in the desert, the forest or by the restless ocean, looking up at the stars, man breathes forth these words, "With only my Maker and me."

The Path
to Prosperity

HE HEALING OF CONDITIONS IS no different from
other healing. All healing is the constructive use of a
mental law which the world is gradually beginning to understand something of. Again we must reiterate the principle of all life. We are surrounded by a thinking medium
from which all things come. We think into it; it does the
rest. Since we are thinking beings and cannot stop thinking, and since Creative Mind receives our thought and
cannot stop creating, it must always be making something for us. What it will make depends absolutely and
only upon what we are thinking, and what we will attract
will depend entirely upon our holding thought to the
complete exclusion of all that would contradict it. It is
not enough that we should sit down and say, "I am one
with Infinite Life." This must mean more than mere
words; it must be felt, it must become an embodiment of
a positive mental attitude. It is not claiming something
to be true which is going to happen; it is not sending out
an aspiration, or a desire, or a supplication, or a prayer; it
must be the embodiment of that which knows that *now it*

is. This is more than holding a thought. Our ability to attract will depend upon the largeness of our thought as we feel that it flows out into a great Universal Creative Power. We are dealing with the form in thought, and not with the form in matter. We have learned that when we get the true form in thought and permeate it with the spirit of belief we will see the thought made flesh without any further effort on our part.

Thought can attract to us only that which we first mentally embody. We cannot attract to ourselves that which we are not. We can attract in the outer only that which we have first completely mentally embodied within, that which has become a part of our mental make-up, a part of our inner understanding.

A man going into business will attract to himself that which he thinks about the most. If he is a barber he will attract people who want to be shaved or have their hair cut. If he sells shoes he will attract people who want to buy shoes. (See *Creative Mind and Success* by the author of the present volume.) So it is with everything; we will not only do this, but we will also attract as much of anything as we mentally embody. This is apt to be overlooked in the study of metaphysics. It is not enough to say that we attract what we think; *we become what we think,* and what we become we will attract.

Do not become merely sentimental about this. Your life is governed by more than a sentiment; it is governed by law, something that cannot be broken, something that picks up every mental attitude and does something with it.

This fundamental proposition of the law should then work out into our conditions. Always remember that it does just as we think. It does not argue, it simply does the thing *as* we think it. Now how are we thinking? Never ask a patient how he is feeling; ask, how are you thinking today? This is the only thing that matters. How are we thinking about life and our conditions? Are we receiving the race suggestion; are we saying that there is not enough to go around? If we are saying this, it is our belief, and there is something that will see that it becomes a part of our expression. Most people, through ignorance of the higher laws of their being, are suffering from the thoughts imposed upon them from a negative and doubtful world. We who are claiming the use of the greater law must emancipate ourselves from all sense of limitation. We are not to be governed by the outer confusion but by the inner realization. We are to judge life not from the way that things in the past have been done, but from the way that the Spirit does things.

The Way
of the Spirit

*A*GAIN LET US SAY THAT THE SPIRIT creates by becoming the thing that it thinks. There is no other possible way in which it could work. Since it is all and there is no other, the thought of opposing forces never enters into its mental working; when we are judging from the outer we are not working in line with the power that we should be using. We must come to see that there is only *One Power* and that we are touching it at all points, for there is not a power of poverty and a power of prosperity. There is the one becoming the many; it makes and it unmakes that a higher form may appear to express through it. All that is not in line with its forward movement will soon pass away, for it recognizes no opposite. As far as we are concerned what we are and what we are to become depends only upon what we are thinking, for this is the way that we are using creative power. The sooner we get away from the thought that we have to create, the sooner we will be able to work in line with the Spirit. Always man uses; he never creates anything. The united intelligence of the human race could not make a single rosebud; it does not know enough. But our slightest thought adrift in mind causes the same power that makes all things to create for us. The great error of the race is, and always has been, that men have thought to give a physical reason for things. When that reason has not answered the problems of life they have sought out some other reason just as physical. The fact that they are all wrong is shown in that every generation has found a different reason. When truth is found it will also be found that it never changes to suit the whims of the human fancy. This is proven by the fact that whatever of the real truth the race has discovered has never been changed. The truth that was revealed to the prophets of old has never changed; it is the same today as it was thousands of years ago. Whoever touches truth, no matter in what generation, will always get the same answer. The great truth that was revealed from Moses to the time of Jesus is the same truth that is still revealed to all who will accept it; it is simply this: we are now living in a Spiritual Universe governed by mental laws of cause and effect. Moses saw it mostly from the standpoint of the Law of cause and effect, an eye for an eye. What does this mean? It means, as Jesus said, "As a man sows, so shall he reap." Moses saw the law. Jesus saw not only the law ("I am come not to destroy but to fulfill"), but he saw behind the law the reason for it, and revealed behind all law the Great Law-giver, a God of love working out the great inner concepts of His own being in harmony and in beauty, filled with peace,

causing the sun to shine alike upon the just and the un-
just. Jesus did not try to overcome the use of law; He understood all law and He well knew that all law was at His
command; He did not break the law, He fulfilled it. So we
must find that all is at our command through these same
laws. The man who understands law and complies with it
will have no difficulty in demonstrating that it is as true
for him as it ever was for anyone else. What, then, are the
laws underlying prosperity? The first is this, and we must
not try to escape it: "Thou shalt have no other Gods before me." This Me is Spirit. We are, then, to trust only in
the activity of Spirit for what we need. But the world will
say, "Human things come through human agencies." This
may be true, but we must realize that the power we are
dealing with also has within its own mind all people and
all things. We do not have to treat people; what we have to
do is to embody principle. Principle may use people, but
that is no part of our responsibility. Ultimately all is Spirit, and Spirit which is the beginning is also the end of all
manifestation. "I am the Alpha and the Omega."' Our
life, then, is to be governed by Spirit. We need look no
further. It will do for us all that we will ever ask, provided
we believe. Why, then, has it not done so? The answer is
that it has already done so, but we have not received it.
The Spirit may offer, but we must accept the gift before it
can be made. "Behold, I stand at the door and knock." We
must understand that this receiving is a mental process; it
is one of mentally taking.

The way, then, that we are using mind through our thought is the way that we are treating ourselves for prosperity. So simple, and yet we have not understood it! If a man says, "I have not," he will not receive; if he says, "I have," he will receive. "To those who have shall be given, and to those who have not shall be taken away even that which they have." This is a veiled statement of the law of cause and effect. When you send out into mind the thought that you have not, it accepts the idea and takes away from you even that which you have. Reverse the process and say, "I have," and it will at once set to work to create for you even more than you now possess. You will readily see then that you are not dealing with two powers but with one, and that it operates through your own thought, doing unto all even as they believe.

The Level
of Consciousness

SINCE ALL IS MIND, AND IT IS done unto us as we mentally think, all life is simply a law of thought—activity of consciousness. In our life the power flows through us. If we provide a big receptivity, it will do a big thing; if, on the other hand, we only believe in a small way, the activity must be a small one. The Spirit can do for us only what it can do through us. Unless we are able to provide the consciousness, it cannot make the gift. Few people have a great consciousness, and this explains why so few excel. The power behind all things of itself is without limit; it is all-power; in us it has to become what we make it. We carry within our own soul the key to all expression, but few enter in. The door is not seen with the physical eye, and as yet but few have gained the ability to see; the majority merely look. Realizing, then, that while the power is limitless it must become operative through our own thought, we shall see that what we need is not some greater power, but that what we really need is a greater consciousness, a deeper realization of life, a grander concept of being. We must unify ourselves with the great whole. The man who dares to fling his thought out into universal intelligence with the positive assurance of one who knows and dares to claim all there is will find that it will be done. God will honor his request. On the other hand, the one who fears to speak lest God will smite will find himself smitten of the law, not because God is angry, but because it is done as he believes.

We have a right to have and should expect to have in this world all that will make for the comfort and for the luxuries of life. What matter how much we have, if we rob no other soul to get it? Shall not the Power that so lavishly spreads Itself out into nature give to us Its highest expression, all that we can ask? We dishonor God when we claim less than all. Until we can expand our thought so that we shall be able to say also, "*I am,*" we need not expect to get great results.

The soul that knows its own Divinity is the great soul; before it all else must bend; to it all else must gravitate. Enlarge your thought processes. Away with the little personal thoughts of things, and dare to think in universal terms about all things. The universe is running over with good, it is for you, but you must believe and then take it. Do you dare to believe that your own word is invincible? When you speak it how do you feel? Is it limitless, is it all power, is all power given to you in heaven and on earth. are you one with the only power that there is? Until you can say yes to all these questions and not simply believe them but *know* them, you cannot hope to attain. It is useless in making a demonstration to beg for things; as well beg that water should be wet or that fire should be hot. Things are, we must take them. Your word has only the power that you put into it, no more and no less. We are all held accountable for every word that we speak because all is the action and the reaction of mind. Man is his own heaven and his own hell.

We start a new enterprise and wonder what the chances of success are; have we realized that the outer is simply the inner manifested? When we go to a new place we shall find there only what we have taken with us. If we have taken success we will find success; if, on the other hand, we have taken failure we will find failure. This is the law; none can avoid it, none need try. Every living soul is a law unto his own life. "There is no law but my own soul shall set." Nothing can come upon the path of the soul but that thing that the soul attracts.

Practice for Prosperity

*P*ROSPERITY IS IN OUR OWN HANDS to do with as
we will, but we will never reach it until we learn to
control our thought We must see only what we want and
never allow the other things to enter. If we wish activity
we must be active in our thought, we must see activity
and speak it into everything that we do. The spoken word
shall bring it to pass. We speak the word, it is brought to
pass of the Power that we speak it into. We can only speak
the word that we understand, the activity will correspond
to our inner concepts. If they are large the results will
be large. The thing to do is to unify ourselves with all
the biggest ideas that we can compass; and realizing that
our ideas govern our power of attraction, we should be
constantly enlarging within ourselves. We must realize
our at-one-ment with All Power and know that our word
will bring it to pass. We speak the word, it is brought to
pass. As consciousness grows it will manifest in enlarged
opportunities and a greater field of action. Most people
think in the terms of universal powers. Feel that you are
surrounded by all the power that there is when you speak

and never doubt but that what you say will spring into being.

We should speak right out into mind all that we desire, and believe that it will be done unto us. Never take the time to listen to those who doubt. We observe that their philosophy has done but little to save the world or themselves. Here again let the dead bury the dead and see to it that you maintain in your own thought what you want, letting go of all else. Think only what you want to happen and never let yourself get mentally lazy and sluggish taking on the suggestions of poverty and limitation. See yourself as being in the position that you desire, mentally dwell upon it and then speak with perfect assurance that it is done; and then forget it and trust in the law. This will answer all needs. If you want to do this for someone else, all that you will need to do is to think of them and go through the same process of mind action. You will be sending out the truth for them, and mind being always active will not contradict what you have said.

Remember that you cannot hope to get results unless you keep but the *one* idea and do not mix thoughts in your mind. All is yours, but you must take it. The taking is always a mental process; it is believing absolutely. This is divine principle.

Conclusion

PRINCIPLE ITSELF IS SIMPLICITY, yet it is infinite—it is Infinite Mind and manifestation of Mind. We live in a Spiritual universe governed through thought, or the word which first becomes law; this law creates what we call matter. Jesus Christ discerned the truth about spiritual principles more than any other man who ever lived, and he proclaimed the eternal reign of law and understanding, absolute, complete, perfect; and he found that law to be operative through his own thought and the power of his own word. And when you and I shall cease looking outside ourselves to any person and shall realize that whatever truth and whatever power we shall have must flow through us; when we begin to interpret our own natures, we shall begin to understand God and law, and life, and not until then.

We live and move and have our being in what we call an Infinite Mind, an Infinite Creative Mind, also infinitely receptive, operative, omnipotent, and all-knowing; and we have learned that this mind presses against us on all sides, flows through us, and becomes operative through our thinking. The human race, ignorant of the laws of this mind, ignorant of the power of its own thought, has through its ignorance misused and abused the creative power of its thought, and brought upon itself the thing it feared. This is true because all thought is law, and all law is mind in action, and the word which you speak today is the law which shall govern your life tomorrow, as the word which you spoke, ignorantly or innocently, consciously or unconsciously yesterday, is absolutely governing your life today. As metaphysicians, then, we are not dealing with a material, nor denying a manifest universe, but we are claiming that the manifestation is the result of the inner activity of the mind; and if we wish for a definite manifestation, we must produce a definite inner activity. *You and I, then, are not dealing with conditions, but with mental and spiritual law.* We are dealing with the power of thought, the power of mind, and the more spiritual the thought the higher the manifestation. The more our reliance upon what we call God, the greater the power.

It is the new education because it strips all the false from the old belief and reveals the individual. It is the new age, because as sure as God is, it will usher in and express the perfect life, the revelation of this truth, and our ability to use it; and it is your own fault when you know this and do not prove it.

If, knowing the infinite power flowing through you, you still remain sick and unhappy, miserable and poor, my friend, it is your own fault. Do not blame God, do not blame man, and do not say it is of the devil. *It is your own fault.* Every time you say *I Am,* you are recognizing the eternal infinite presence of omnipotent power within yourself, which is God operating through your thought, and that is why you bring upon yourself the thing you fear, and why you bring to yourself the thing you want.

When fifty-one percent of your thinking is health and life and power, that day the fifty-one percent will swallow up, erase, kill out the rest. The day you, as an individual, through fifty-one percent of your thought, pass beyond the perception of limitation, you will draw out of the universe everything you desire; poverty will desert you and you will be emancipated forever. The day you think fifty-one percent of happiness, misery shall depart and never return. Is it not then worth your time and your effort, and should it not be the greatest purpose in the life of any awakened soul so to depict this principle as to emancipate himself?

The way can be shown, but each individual must himself walk the way. We are so bound by suggestion and hypnotized by false belief, so entangled by the chaotic thinking of the world, thinking which is based upon the principle of a dual mind, that we become confused and are not ourselves. Wake up! Your word is all-powerful, your consciousness is one with Omnipotence. Your thought is infinite. Your destiny is eternal and your home is everlasting heaven. Realize the truth—I am liv-

ing in a perfect universe, it always was perfect and always
will be perfect. There never was a mistake made, there are
no mistakes being made, and there never will be. I live in
the great and eternal universe of perfection from cause to
effect, from beginning to end, and "The world's all right,
and I know it."

Majestic and calm, waiting with eternal and divine
patience, the Great Principle of Life is ready to give to us
all that it has. And while we listen and wait we will cast
from us everything that hinders its complete expression
through us, we will let go of all struggle and all strife and
be at peace with Life.

Perfect peace to the soul as we rest in the realization
of our unity with all that there is, was or ever will be. One
with the Infinite Mind. All the power of the Spirit is
working through our thought as we believe and receive.
Now we will ask for and take that thing which we desire;
it is done, it is complete, now and forever. Perfect life,
perfect healing, perfect harmony, Divine guidance, Infinite strength and joy forever.

Questions and Answers

What is the Truth?
The Truth is that which is. It is all that is. As there cannot be
something and nothing, so the Truth, being that which is. must
at the same time be all that there is.

Where is the Truth?
If the Truth is All, it must be everywhere; being all, there is no
other substance to divide it with; being undivided, it is everywhere present. All Truth, which means all power, must be present at all points, or at any given point, at any and at all times.

Has the Truth changed?
A substance cannot change unless there is something for it to
change into. Since the Truth is all, it cannot change, for there
is no other thing for it to change into; whatever is the Truth,
then, has never changed.

Is the Truth, or that which is, one or many?
It must be one, since it is all.

Is the Truth conscious?
Yes, man is conscious. He could not be so unless Truth or Life
were conscious. Man's self-consciousness proves the self-consciousness of Life or Truth or Spirit. Like produces like.

What comes out of life?

Everything that is comes out of life. If life is all then it follows that all that is is some form of life.

How does Life make things?

Being all, it must make things out of itself. It must operate upon itself, through itself, and out of itself must make all that is made. Being conscious, It must know that it is doing this.

What would we call this inner movement of Life?

The inner movement of Life or consciousness we would call thought or the self-knowing of Life or Spirit.

Then the universe and all that is a part of it comes from thought?

Yes, everything comes from thought.

Do we not see a visible world that seems to change, and if we do, how is it that it could come from something that never changes?

Yes, we do see a changing world, but back of it is a changeless substance. The thing that changes is the thought or form; the substance from which this form comes never changes. It is one and undivided, and takes form through thought in all things. We prove this when we resolve all things into one source. All material things, so called, can be reduced into formless substance, the sole activity of which must be thought or the movement of intelligence upon itself.

What causes form to change?

The intelligence behind it.

Is there nothing in the universe, then, but Life, thought and form?

These are all.

If this is true, what is physical law?

Physical law is simply the result of the inner movement of Life.

If things and laws are the result of the inner movement of Life, then does it not follow that thoughts are things?

Yes, all things are simply thought forms.

How long does thought last as form?

As long as the thought is held in Life or Mind.

Does the thought of Life, Mind or Good ever change?

From all that we can know the thought of God seems to change. That is, planets change, take form and again become formless. When we realize that all this can take place without ever changing the substance behind it, we see no reason why God's thought could not change and ever build up a higher form. Indeed, this is one of the teachings of Ancient Wisdom, that while reality never changes, the form that it takes is ever changing.

What is man's place in the creative order?

Man is a thinking center in Mind, reproducing in a smaller scale all there is in the Universe.

Does this not make man's thought creative?

In a certain sense it does. What we call creation is not making something out of nothing, but it is thought taking form. And as man thinks, and as thought must take form, then it must follow that man's thought must take form in mind and so become creative.

What is man's thought?

It is the activity of that something within that can say, "I Am."

What is the difference between God and man?

The very fact that man can say, "I Am," proves that he is. Since he is he must be made out of life and must be some part of all that there is. This being so, man must be a part of God's consciousness. The difference would be in degree only. He must be as much of Life as he recognizes himself to be.

Is all of man's thought creative?

Yes, all or none. If one thought produces, then all must.

If this be true, how is it that man seems to be so limited?

Because he has thought limitation, and thoughts are things and will always make the thing thought of. In reality the very fact that man's thought can limit him also proves that it could free him from all limitation by simply changing his thought.

But why is man so made that he can think two ways?

This is a question that can be answered only in one way. Unless a man can think as he wants to think he would not be a man at all but simply a piece of mechanism. Man is an individual and that means self choice, backed by a power that will produce the thing chosen. In discovering himself man chooses many things, uses them and passes to a higher choice, ever ascending in the scale of being. As fast as he chooses, he experiences that thing which he thinks about.

What is evil?

Evil is the result of a lack of clear seeing, based upon a belief in two powers, and limitation and what we call sin is the result of man's struggle to find himself.

If this be true, why could we not at once begin to change our whole life by first changing our thought?

We could. We would not be changing real substance, but we would be changing the form that it takes through our thought. All that we can change is the form of thought through which experiences come to us.

What is the limit of man's creative use of Mind?

Man is limited by nothing but his own thinking, by his mental ability to conceive.

What is meant by mental conception?

All things are produced by thought. The thing produced from mind is first formed in thought; thought molds mind into form.

But do we not have to act?

We cannot think without acting; an inactive body is the result of an inactive mind.

In using our creative powers, how far do we have to consider the conditions under which we live?

We do not have to consider them at all. Conditions are the result, the effect and not the cause; we create them as fast as we think.

How would a person start to change conditions?

By first changing thought and by realizing that we are not deal-ing with an illusion, but with the great reality. Then by acting as though we already have what we think.

How long would it take to do this?

As long as it would take to let go of all negative thought and embody all positive thought. This would depend entirely upon the individual and his mental ability to control thought.

What would hinder us the most?

Ourselves; no one gives to us but ourselves and no one takes from us but ourselves.

Can no one else help us?

Only to a limited degree. While we may be helped by those who understand the law, for a time, yet sooner or later we must our-selves take the creative responsibility of our own lives. Others may think for us for a few moments a day, but we think for our-selves all the time.

But does not God help us?

Yes, God helps all, but must do it through law. "All's love yet all's law."

How should we pray?

By giving thanks that we already have that thing that we pray for; by completely believing and by never doubting. "When ye pray believe that ye have received and ye shall receive." We must be sure that in no way shall we think, act or talk or read about limitation. We must all be a law unto ourselves.

Definitions

Absolute. Complete self-knowing.

Attraction. The drawing power of thought.

Causation. God, Spirit, Life. That which is.

Consciousness. The realization of the fact that we are.

Creation. Thought becoming form. The Immaculate Conception.

Demonstration. The result of correct thinking.

Effect. The result of inner motion.

Faith. Positive mental activity.

Fear. Negative mental activity.

God. Infinite Spirit, self-knowing Mind, Life, Truth, Intelligence, Love, All Cause and All Effect. That invisible power which makes all things out of Itself, by an inner action of its own thought upon Itself.

Health. The realization of perfect life.

Heaven. The atmosphere of correct thought.

Hell. The atmosphere of false thinking.

Illusion. Belief in two powers.

Intelligence. That which knows that it is.

Karma. The law of cause and effect. The result of past thought and action binding the ignorant and freeing the wise.

Law. Mind in action; law is not cause, it is effect. It is intelligence operating. All law is universal.

Life. Consciousness of power and activity.

Man. A thinking center in mind.

Motion. The inner activity of life producing manifestation.

Multiplicity. The bringing forth from the One of an infinite variety of form, color and motion.

Objective. Life in its outer form.

Peace. Mind resting in the realization that it is all.

Poise. An inner calm which never fears.

Poverty. Limited thought.

Power. The result of the union of peace and poise.

Realization. An inner thought process whereby we become conscious of our unity with life.

Riches. The realization of our unity with life, which is limitless.

Righteousness. Spiritual understanding.

Sense. Not an illusion, but the faculties through which we contact life in its expression.

Sickness. Image of thought held in mind appearing on the body.

Sin. Lack of understanding.

Soul. The inner creative life, the feminine, receptive, creative.

Subjective. Life in its inner thought or form.

The Visible Universe. The ideas of God in expression, the body of God, expression of the Divine Mind. All visible life is an expression of an inner concept.

The Word. The activity of thought.

Thought. The activity of Mind.

Treatment. The mental and spiritual activity of thought for a definite end.

Truth. That which is.

Unfoldment. The birth of ideas coming forth from Mind.

Unity. One Mind flowing through all, and in all.

Vibration. Not intelligence, but the result of intelligence, it follows cause.

About the Author

Ernest Shurtleff Holmes was born in 1887 on a farm near Lincoln, Maine. At the age of twenty-five, he moved to California to be with his brother Fenwick, who had established a small church in the community of Venice, a suburb of Los Angeles, and to carve out a life of his own. Holmes was both a gifted thinker and speaker—his ideas on spirituality and life challenged and inspired his audiences to think for themselves.

In 1919, Holmes published his first book, *Creative Mind*. In 1926, he published his seminal work, *The Science of Mind*. In the following year, he founded the Institute of Religious Science and School of Philosophy and its monthly magazine *Science of Mind*. As his lecture series continued to grow in popularity and his ideas took root, more and more Religious Science ministries were established throughout the country. In 1949, Dr. Holmes could be heard each Sunday on the Mutual Network, broadcasting his words of hope and inspiration from coast to coast. In 1953, the Institute was renamed the Church of Religious Science and Philosophy—later to become the United Church of Religious Science, with member churches throughout the world.

By the time of his passing in 1960, Ernest Holmes had left a wealth of knowledge through his many books, study courses, and recordings, and the legacy of a living philosophy that allowed people to understand their true nature and achieve their individual goals in life.

AS A MAN DOES
Morning and Evening Thoughts

James Allen

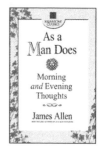

One of the first great modern writers of motivational and inspirational books, James Allen has influenced millions of people around the world through books like *As a Man Thinketh*. In the same way, *As a Man Does: Morning and Evening Thoughts* presents beautiful and insightful meditations to feed the mind and soul.

In each of the sixty-two meditations—one for each morning and each evening of the month—Allen offers both the force of truth and the blessing of comfort. Whether you are familiar with the writings of James Allen or you have yet to read any of his stirring books, this beautiful volume is sure to move you, console you, and inspire you—every morning and every evening of your life.

$8.95 • 144 pages • 5.5 x 8.5-inch quality paperback • 2-color • Inspiration/Religion • ISBN 0-7570-0018-5

LIGHT ON LIFE'S DIFFICULTIES
Illuminating the Paths Ahead

James Allen

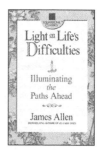

James Allen is considered to be one of the first great modern writers of motivational and inspirational books. Today, his work *As a Man Thinketh* continues to influence millions around the world. In the same way, this newly discovered classic, *Light on Life's Difficulties,* offers twenty-three beautiful and insightful essays. Readers will find that each essay contains both the force of truth and the blessing of comfort.

In a time of crisis, *Light on Life's Difficulties* offers clear direction to those on a search for personal truths. In Allen's own words, "This book is intended to be a strong and kindly companion, as well as a source of spiritual renewal and inspiration. It will help its readers transform themselves into the ideal characters they would wish to be."

Light on Life's Difficulties is designed to shed light on those areas of our lives that we have become uncertain about—areas such as spirituality, self-control, individual liberty, war and peace, sorrow, and so much more. Although written almost one hundred years ago, the power of Allen's words can and will illuminate the road ahead for so many of us.

$8.95 • 128 pages • 5.5 x 8.5-inch quality paperback • 2-Color • Inspiration/Religion • ISBN 0-7570-0040-1

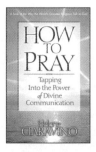

HOW TO PRAY

Tapping Into the Power of Divine Communication

Helene Ciaravino

The power of prayer is real. It can heal illness, win battles, and move personal mountains. Cultures and religions throughout the world use their own individual systems of divine communication for comfort, serenity, guidance, and more. *How to Pray* was written for everyone who wants to learn more about this universal practice.

How to Pray begins by widening your perspective on prayer through several intriguing definitions. It then discusses the many scientific studies that have validated the power of prayer, and—to shine a light on any roadblocks that may be hindering you—it discusses common reasons why some people don't pray. Part Two examines the history and prayer techniques of four great traditions: Judaism, Christianity, Islam, and Buddhism. In these chapters, you'll learn about the beliefs, practices, and individual prayers that have been revered for centuries. Part Three focuses on the development of your own personal prayer life, first by explaining some easy ways in which you can make your practice of prayer more effective and fulfilling, and then by exploring the challenges of prayer—from seemingly unanswered prayers and spiritual dry spells, to the joyful task of making your whole day a prayer. Finally, a useful resource directory suggests books and websites that provide further information.

$13.95 • 264 pages • 6 x 9-inch quality paperback • Inspiration/Self-Help • ISBN 0-7570-0012-6

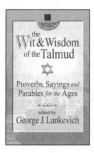

THE WIT AND WISDOM OF THE TALMUD

Proverbs, Sayings, and Parables for the Ages

Edited by George J. Lankevich

In Jewish tradition, the Talmud embodies the laws of Judaism, as well as a way of study and intellectual development. Composed of two works, the Mishnah and the Gemara, the Talmud is believed to provide serious students with one of the most sacred of experiences. It is, in fact, the Torah—the Old Testament—and the Talmud that offer the tenets of the Jewish religion.

Here, in this classic work—representing almost two thousand years of learning—are those pearls of wisdom that we can all benefit from and enjoy time and time again. Some may be familiar to you; others may be new. All, however, can offer illuminating insights and direction throughout your life.

$13.95 • 160 pages • 5.5 x 8.5-inch quality paperback • 2-color • Religion/Judaism • ISBN 0-7570-0021-5

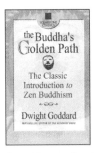

THE BUDDHA'S GOLDEN PATH
The Classic Introduction to Zen Buddhism
Dwight Goddard

In 1929, when author Dwight Goddard wrote *The Buddha's Golden Path*, he was breaking ground. No American before him had lived the lifestyle of a Zen Buddhist monk, and then set out to share the secrets he had learned with his countrymen. This title was the first American book published to popularize Zen Buddhism. Released in the midst of the Great Depression, in its own way, it offered answers to the questions that millions of disillusioned people were beginning to ask—questions about what was really important in their lives. Questions we still ask ourselves today.

As a book of instruction, *The Buddha's Golden Path* has held up remarkably well. As a true classic, it has touched countless lives, and has opened the door for future generations in this country to study and embrace the principles of Zen.

$14.95 • 208 pages • 5.5 x 8.5-inch quality paperback • 2-color • Religion/Zen Buddhism • ISBN 0-7570-0023-1

TAO TE CHING
The Way of Virtue
Lao Tzu • Translated by Patrick Michael Byrne

The *Tao Te Ching* has served as a personal road map for millions of people. It is said that its words reveal the underlying principles that govern the world in which we live. Holding to the laws of nature—drawing from the essence of what all things are—it offers both a moral compass and an internal balance. A fundamental book of the Taoist, the *Tao Te Ching* is regarded as a revelation in its own right. For those seeking a better understanding of themselves, it provides a wealth of wisdom and insights.

Through time—from one powerful dynasty to another—many changes have been made to the original Chinese text of the *Tao Te Ching*. Over the last century, translators have added to the mix by incorporating their interpretations. For those readers who are looking for a purer interpretation of the *Tao Te Ching*, researcher Patrick Michael Byrne has produced a translation that is extremely accurate, while capturing the pattern and harmony of the original. Here is a *Tao Te Ching* that you can enjoy, understand, and value.

$10.95 • 128 pages • 5.5 x 8.5-inch quality paperback • 2-color • Religion/Chinese • ISBN 0-7570-0029-0